MAN TALK

—THE BOOK—

"The Hard Things Men Never Talk About"

Chris Howell

1 to 12 to 12 to 12
Who do you talk to all the time
TDS 12-08-04

inner humility strengthens
low expectations - cripple
be around people that demand more of you
become great by finding the thing
Aaron's mistakes helped him find the criteria for the job
No fruitfulness w/o relationship
Add dignity to what other people think is needed, a city,
small things w/ excellence is a sign of greatness.
Get in under that make you feel stupid
Listen while you dress
If your name is attached to it
Let it Be Excellent

Man Talk

(The Book)

"The Hard Things That Men Never Talk About"

by

Chris Howell

Unless otherwise indicated, all Scripture quotations contained herein are taken from the *King James Version* of the Bible.

The Scripture quotation marked NIV is taken from *The Holy Bible: New International Version.* Copyright © 1973, 1978, 1984 by The International Bible Society. Used by permission of Zondervan Bible Publishers.

Man Talk (The Book)
"The Hard Things That Men Never Talk About"
ISBN0-9622860-5-2
Copyright © 2004 by
Chris Howell
P. O. Box 300284
Arlington, TX 76007

Typesetter: Lisa Simpson
Artist: David Wilson
Editor: Marilyn L. Price

Printed in the United States of America. All rights reserved under International Copyright Law. Contents and/or cover may not be reproduced in whole or in part in any form without the express written consent of the Publisher.

Published by Whole Armour Publishing
P.O. Box 223722
Dallas, TX 75222-3722

Dedication

I dedicate this book to:

My son, Christopher J. Howell Jr.

My brother, Cedric D. Howell

Contents

Acknowledgments 9

Introduction 11

Chapter 1   Men and Communication 15

Chapter 2   Men and Sex 27

Chapter 3   Men and Relationships 47

Chapter 4   Men and Emotions 55

Chapter 5   Men – As Fathers 67

Chapter 6   Men and Money 79

Conclusion 87

Prayer of Salvation 91

Acknowledgments

To properly give thanks to all of the people who have impacted my life or have in some way contributed to this project, it would take more pages than what I am allotted here. So let me just say thank you to all of my family and many friends.

To those who are so close I must name specifically:

My wife, Lady Dominique Howell, I really appreciate all of your words of encouragement, your listening ear, oh, and your money to help bring this project to fruition. Seriously, you are truly what God was thinking of when He said it is not good for Chris to be alone. He designed me a helpmeet and you do your job well. I love you!

To the only three people on this earth whom I get the privilege of calling my children: Christina, Dominique, and Chris Jr. I thank you for your words of encouragement. Your belief in me gives me the motivation and inspiration to keep on keeping on. My strongest desire is to see you become all that God has ordained you to be.

To my mother, Ms. Annie P. Howell, thank you for consistently encouraging me to stay the course, not only in your words to me but in the example that you have set before in singlehandedly raising six children. It is this that has always served as a great source of inspiration for me in the tough times. I have always been able to count on you to cheer me on and encourage me to stay in the game and for that I am forever grateful. We scored!!!

Thanks to Elder Raymond Orr and his lovely wife, Patrice, for taking my family under your wings and serving as examples of a great man and woman of God. Also, thanks for encouraging us to dream.

Thanks to Melissa Norris for your words of wisdom, insight, and literary expertise that you contributed to this project. It means a lot.

Thanks to Marilyn Price, Lisa Simpson, and David Wilson you all are the best in the business and I greatly appreciate your contributions to this project.

Introduction

Men have been raised by parents, conditioned by society, and often encouraged by women to play the roles of lover, husband, parent, breadwinner, and strong and silent man. All of these impossible demands psychologically cripple and eventually physically kill them.

The book that you now hold in your hands is a result of conversations that I have been blessed and privileged to share with thousands of men in "Men Only" talk sessions. Men are no longer silent about the issues that are threatening our world. In these sessions, we address the issues in a man's world. And guaranteed, these issues will not go away until we face them, address our level of concern, and find solutions for them.

This may sound selfish when our young people are dropping out of high school at record numbers and filling up our penal institutions at an even greater rate. Women are now taking on more responsibilities than ever before. Drugs are infiltrating our communities, both urban and suburban neighborhoods. Guns and gang violence are at an all-time high. It appears as if our young people have lost regard for human life. These are all very serious issues and need to be addressed.

But the deeper, even more pressing issue for me right now, is that the vast majority of us as men are having a hard time saving our families, communities, and society as a whole because we are fighting wars within ourselves. So it is with my "Man Talk" sessions where thousands of men have come to try and find answers to some of life's most difficult questions regarding the issues in a man's world.

Men's lives have been impacted by conversations we have had about issues in their lives. With this same intent, this book came about. In it we address the hard issues in a man's world that we've never talked about until now and attempt to offer some solutions to help improve in these areas.

If you are a man, you will certainly identify and gain some insight from the issues discussed in this book.

If you are a woman, you will want to read it too so both you and your mate can address and hopefully resolve the issues that exist in your relationship.

◆ **"Now speak or be forever silent."**
Phillip Massinger

Chapter One

Men and Communication

I was sitting with a few buddies after watching a game. It was getting late, the food and the drinks were gone, and we had bragged about everything we could imagine. We had cracked all of the jokes on each other that we could think of when one of them sighed and said, "I guess I have to go home now and pretend to listen to my wife while she rattles on and on about something I won't understand anyway."

Later, as I thought about what he had said, I began to think about how many times other guys have made the same comment regarding their wives and communication.

As common as this is among men in relationships, we have done little to bridge our communication gap with women – until recently. For men, proactive communication with women has been saying whatever it takes to keep them happy whenever possible. We never gave much thought to the fact that there could be such benefits to using more words, especially when they are used to help women understand us better, and help us to understand ourselves better.

In the *American Heritage Student Dictionary,* "communication" is defined as the exchange of thoughts, information, or message by speech, signals, or writing.

In recent years, more studies have focused on the communication of men than ever before. Since scientists in the fields of archeology and psychology began to study the history of mankind and human behavior and analyze modes of communication through time and cultures, they found that men expressed themselves differently than women in every culture since the beginning of recorded time.

Within the last two decades, psychologists, counselors, and ministers found the greatest significance in studying the communication of men and their misinterpretation by women. Professionals have found a virtual language barrier between men and women, previously perceived as a common difference between the sexes. Finally, we have professionals in behavioral science who have studies that prove that men do communicate. We are just wired to do it differently than women. It's sort of like we have our own unwritten language passed down through centuries like a verbal history.

Just the Facts

As men, we have always known that women talk more than we do, but we never gave it as much thought before. We simply accepted it as a fact of life and compared how hard it was to listen to the detailed stories our wives and girlfriends told us to see who had to endure the most grueling details. It was said best in the television series, "Dragnet" – "Just the facts, ma'am. Just the facts."

Men are mentally wired for interests only in the facts, the major occurrences in a sequence of events, and not the many minute details women find so important to include. Those who have given their efforts to the study of people and relationships generally concur that men and women do not communicate in the same ways. When a woman asks you, "How was your day?" you can summarize a full eight-hour day, lunch, and your morning and evening commute in one or two words: "all right," "horrible," "okay," "lousy," or "fine." Some men can say a lot in less than a word. A grunt or a sigh can speak volumes.

Cause and Effect

Perhaps it is because women are innately more nurturing than we are that they tend to approach most situations as a cause and effect fact-finding mission. For example, at the sound of a crying baby, a woman, especially the mother, will ask, "What's wrong? Why are you crying?" Then, she will search the baby from head to toe and its surroundings until she assesses the need, or finds the offending culprit.

On the other hand, we as the father will wonder why the baby is crying and jump into action to do something, anything to console the baby and stop its crying. So, often the baby is crying and we as men and fathers are trying to give him or her a bottle, or calm the baby with a toy rattle. Or we will even resort to making silly faces and embarrassing noises to quiet the baby, only to discover that the diaper we changed thirty minutes ago is full of a mess that would make a grown man cry. It needs to be changed again!

Why After Why

Women, unlike men, are more often concerned with the cause and effect, and everything in between. It's the focus on "everything in between" that men would rather not hear about, and women feel incomplete without. Women use the word "why" and/or end a sentence with a question more often than we do. They have an insatiable need to know things and ask questions.

Ask most women the first time, or the second, why they want to know every little detail and why they ask so many questions, and most of them find it difficult to articulate. They just know that they have a drive, an absolute need to know. Other women have told me that their need to know is associated with their need to feel close, as close as if they were there with you when everything happened. Since they were not there, they want to experience it and try to fully comprehend everything vicariously through every detail they can get.

Much like many women enjoy reading a novel or a romance novel chuck full of descriptive details down to the stride of the steps of the leading romance character as he entered the room, or even the colors and design of the wallpaper in a room, that helps them to visualize the scene as if they were there. The same is true for the details they interrogate us for that we often simply find unnecessary. As men, we tend to condense a full day of information down to sixty seconds of sound bites. Women recant their day more like a thirty- to sixty-minute special report!

Women often ask questions that men do not know quite how to answer readily. First of all, we are so confounded by the idea that we are presented with the question that we have to be reminded to formulate an answer. Often, we are so fixated on and bewildered by how she even came up with the question that it may take us hours or days to get beyond our shock and actually consider the question and derive an answer.

Where we often get tripped up is that since we have less regard for the "why," because we focus on "what is," we tend not to properly distinguish between a rhetorical question and a question we are expected to answer. If we are not experienced enough to impress women with the right answer, or the answer they want, which are one and the same, then either we do not respond, grunt an "I don't know," or we say the wrong thing and worsen the already stressful moment.

Fright or Flight Communication?

I have conducted many "men only" talk sessions. It seems to me that we never really have a problem talking to each other. So why do we often find it difficult to talk to women? You may have heard that men generally have a fear of intimacy. From our all men talk sessions, I would say that it is not so much a fear of "intimacy" as perhaps a fear of "exposure." After all, we have our manly image to protect.

From infancy, we have been groomed to be big and strong, tough and hard. We were told that crying is for girls, so suck it up. When we got hurt playing as children and nothing was broken, we were told to shake it off and get back out there. When we got injured in sports, if nothing was broken and we did not have a concussion, again we were told to shake it off and get back out there.

So, now that we are men, we are best at shaking it off and getting back out there, not nursing our feelings. Feelings have scared us because we have always thought that a guy must be weak if he has any feelings that are not physical or sexual in nature.

The masculine image was too important to us to risk showing a soft side. We thought that women would not respect us, and worse, we thought that other men would think that we were weak. We never knew how much women loved seeing a little emotion from us. *What took us so long for someone to tell us how sexy women find men who can shed a tear in a tender moment?* Many men said that their woman was more passionate after they saw them shed a few tears in sadness. Who knew?

> What took us so long for someone to tell us how sexy women find men who can shed a tear in a tender moment?

We have missed out on a lot of pleasure from a comforting woman while we held back a sad tear. Just for clarity, it still is not cool to blubber during a "chick flick" at the theatre. That is still over the top for a "manly man."

When you get to talking about "emotions," we tend to retreat because we are innately wired to be less emotional than women. We have emotions. We are just not as open and in touch with them as women are. So when something happens to scratch the hard outer surface of our protective male ego covering, we escape falling into the pit called "emotions" by making a run for it. We take flight physically or mentally (in our thoughts).

Usually, a man does not say, "I need to leave before I fall apart." Typically, we do not take the time to assess just what it is we are feeling. We just know that we need to get away to stop whatever it is we are starting to feel, and put a stop to it before some unfamiliar emotional phenomenon happens to us. Often, we can remain in the same room and retreat mentally by engaging in something else, such as watching television or reading the paper.

Communication 101

The purpose for rethinking how we communicate as men is not to try to make us think more like women, as if that were ever possible. Instead, the purpose is to help us as men find the benefits of better communication and provide examples of how we can improve, and tools we can easily employ to improve our relationships and interactions with the women in our lives.

For the indomitable tough guy who needs a little help with the steps in communicating, here is a mini course for you. Try this simple three-step tutorial to help you think your way through to better communication and reduce any fear of "emotions" you may have.

Step 1 - Observation. The first step in improving communication is to pay more attention to as many details as you can tolerate. (You will increase your tolerance for details with use.) Simply make a mental note of whatever you can see and hear and any other sensory perception you are able to notice.

Step 2 - Evaluation. This one is the easiest step. All you have to do is develop an opinion about what you saw, heard, or perceived. You simply decide if you like it or not, or would someone else like it or find it beneficial.

Step 3 - Response. This is the hardest step of all. This is the point where you give a short verbal report of what you observed and how you evaluate its usefulness.

Once you have practiced these steps enough to do them without much effort or without notes, you are then ready to be certified as a "communicator."

◆ "Build me a son...who will be strong enough to know when he is weak and brave enough to face himself when he is afraid."
                    Douglas MacArthur

Chapter Two

Men and Sex

Finally, after centuries of denial, the biological, innate sexual desire of healthy men with sound minds has been confirmed as "normal." For centuries, we have been criticized for being highly sexual creatures and easily stimulated sexually. Someone finally decided to encourage women and the world to accept the male nature as a fact of life. So, women and men should focus on managing this fact of life so we can just get on with this thing called "life."

One of the top two items on most of our lists of priorities and needs is "sex," superceded only by our need for food. Food often takes second place given the choice between the two. I find it interesting that we are all the result of sex, with the exception of approximately twenty years of in vitro-fertilization and one immaculate conception reported centuries ago. Yet one of the "dirtiest," "darkest," and most "secret" things in life is sex.

On the other hand, sex is one of the few things in life that can be as equally beautiful and pleasurable as it can be deviant and deadly. Of course, like most things, used in proper context, it is constructive. Taken out of proper context, it is destructive.

> Like money, sex is the one thing we feel we really do not have enough of, and for some reason we have always been uneasy about admitting this and trying to understand what it is that makes us feel this way.

Most often in my seminar settings with men, we talk about the "lack" of sex in marital relationships and the difficulty of doing without sex outside of the moral ideal of marriage in conventional male/female relationships. Like money, sex is the one thing we feel we really do not have enough of, and for some reason we have always been uneasy about admitting this and trying to understand what it is that makes us feel this way.

The "Men Only" talk sessions are beginning to shed some light on it for us, because as we get together and talk about this, the room lights up and men begin to see that they are not the only ones who feel this way.

It's like you can see the little cartoon bubble above a guy's head with the statement, "I told my wife nothing was wrong with me."

Often, in Christian settings, we always address things from a married perspective. It's like we just assume that since we are married, everyone is married, so there are few conversations that have been directed to the single people particularly as it relates to sex.

I made it a point during our "Men Only" talk sessions to balance the conversation so we can help our single brothers in the audience who incidentally show up in large numbers. So to the single ladies reading this book, I don't say that so you can camp outside the doors of our sessions, but so you know that your future husband may very well be a product of Man Talk. A few unmarried men admit to having sex with women they are dating or living with.

I have yet to have a gay man discuss his sex life openly in a crowd of men who are less likely to be gay. Most often we discuss the struggle of managing an erection that cannot be satisfied with the availability of that certain woman. Or, we spend a few moments acknowledging the possibility of impotence at some point in every man's life who is healthy, thrives past middle age, and many times before middle age.

This is not a "tell all" book, so I can't give away all of the details of what's discussed in these life-changing sessions. But I do want to move on and talk about the "hard sexual things" we hate to address and try to avoid.

The Drive

"A man's children and his garden both reflect the amount of weeding done during the growing season."
Unknown

The normal human sex drive is a natural physiological process of life. Sexual desire is usually a product of puberty. At approximately twelve to fourteen, the pituitary gland begins to secrete growth hormones that give greater physical definition to the body and stimulate hormones in the male testes and in the female ovaries, which control sexual desire. If you can remember, the transformation probably seemed to have happened over a relatively short period of time. Most of us seem to have left school for the summer a kid and started the next school year as a teenager.

It is at this point, and even younger, when boys need proper information from their parents, teachers, and adults who have authority in their lives. So as a father or male figure in a young man's life, it is important that we assume the responsibility of properly educating our young men about their bodies and the importance of keeping sex in its proper context (in a married male and female relationship).

The same is true for girls, but since girls are naturally not as visually stimulated as boys, they do not become tempted with sexually explicit materials at the same rate that boys often do. Not often will you find a group of girls huddled in the corner of the schoolyard or at a park ogling a picture of a nude man. Nor do we see many girls surfing the Internet for nude sites – at least not for sexual gratification.

Girls are not as fascinated with boys' body parts as boys are fascinated with girls' body parts. The same is true for women and men. After all, when was the last time you saw a woman measure anything on her body with a ruler? *Girls and women are much more fascinated by what we say, how we say it, and what we do about what we have said.*

> Girls and women are much more fascinated by what we say, how we say it, and what we do about what we have said.

From preteen to old age, four things drive men sexually: our eyes, our dreams, our experiences, and testosterone. Testosterone is the hormone that kicks in when we reach puberty that begins to cause erections at the most inopportune times. Almost anything can trigger it, such as seeing a female's cleavage in a low-cut blouse, seeing a protruding nipple pressing against thin fabric, seeing a "cutie" in tight jeans, or even just a quick fantasy.

Men of the same age may have very different testosterone levels, which affect their sex drive. Testosterone diminishes with age and causes reduced sexual function and desire and produces impotence.

Interesting to note: Testosterone is also associated with anger and certain abusive behavior. Studies show that some men who become sexual predators can be controlled by medication, which reduces their testosterone level and controls the mental impulses they cannot seem to control. Other men even agree to be castrated to help control their sexual desire and behavior. I note this not to vilify us as men, but because someone is getting this information about men for the first time, and my hope is to help boys and men with education about boys and men – the good, the bad, and the ugly.

Masturbation

Masturbation is so personal that most people will not discuss it at all. Masturbation is a sexual act that until recently, men would only joke about and not admit doing it. Some men and doctors have encouraged men and boys to masturbate to relieve the sexual tension of an erection that will not easily or soon go down. Because masturbation is typically something a man does completely alone and in private to relieve his own sexual tension, it was an encouraged behavior.

More recently, some religious leaders have denounced masturbation as a form of sex outside of marriage, sinful self-indulgence, and paganism. Other religious authorities have acknowledged it as totally private and off limits as long as no one else is affected.

As common as this practice is, there is still quite a bit of shame associated with it. Perhaps it is because "single sex" is the worst part about being single or alone when a man wants sex. There seems to be something denigrating for a man when he wants a woman and does not have one, or can't allure a woman he would want to have sex with.

Masturbation tends to be a gray area for some people. However, sex therapists say that it can become a problem over time for some men who become unable to achieve a climax without masturbating. Other men use pornography to masturbate. This also becomes problematic in time because no woman can compete with the ideal fantasy that pornography can cause a man to create in his mind. This may sound crazy, but certainly no magazine, phone sex, or Internet porn can replace the real thing.

Professionals say what actually happens is that some men become so used to and content with their fantasy that they no longer can perform without artificial stimuli. Some men become addicted to masturbating that they will do so in places other than in the privacy of their homes. Occasionally, the news will report "exhibitionists" who get their thrills by pleasuring themselves in view of others. While some men use masturbation to manage their sexual desire outside of marriage or between relationships, others use it as a mode of perversion.

Since there is no real definitive answer on masturbation in the privacy of one's home, away from children and non-consenting viewers, you have to let your convictions and the following law be your guide:

> **Therefore, I urge you, brothers, in view of God's mercy, to offer your bodies as living sacrifices, holy and pleasing to God – this is your spiritual act of worship. Do not conform any longer to the pattern of this world, but be transformed by the renewing of your mind. Then you will be able to test and approve what God's will is – his good, pleasing and perfect will.**
>
> **Romans 12:1-2** NIV

Impotence

Sometimes we shudder just to say the word "impotence," but I believe that is because of the connotation that our society has placed upon us as men. You see, there are very few men who are really impotent. I say this because the word "impotent" actually means that you are totally incapable of sexual intercourse because you have lost all power. That may not be the case with most guys who have diagnosed themselves and allowed their wives and the hundreds of television commercials that promote sexual enhancement drugs to intimidate them.

We as men are constantly barraged with images and sound bites that promise to help us regain our potency. It could be that this has forced us to become so preoccupied with this that it has placed an even greater stress on us in the bedroom to where it does not make us impotent, but we have lost some power.

Let's look at some other things that may cause you to lose some of that power. First, let's look at the role that our women play in this thing called "impotence."

Many men have reported that they find it difficult to get an erection with their wife or long-time girlfriend, but are easily aroused when involved in an extramarital affair. First, I do not condone the extramarital affair but use this information to look at a deeper issue with impotence.

Research has shown that the penis does have a bit of wisdom in the sense that after being rejected time and time again, it becomes resentful of the woman and senses her negative energy about the sexual encounter. Therefore, it does not become as aroused as it would during a welcoming encounter. Since few men have knowledge of this, we feel that it is easier to say that we have a medical problem or we chuck it up to stress.

In addition to the loss of power, this type of resentment also causes premature ejaculation because in the mind of the man and the penis, we are saying, "Let's get this over with as soon as possible."

Men, our challenge is not so much a medical problem, but more of an intimacy problem. We have to communicate with our mate about her negative feelings towards the encounter and let her know how she plays a vital part in our potency. I am sure you can point out to her the differences of how you performed when she initiated the encounter and compare it to when you had to beg and plead and she finally gave in.

So before you run out to get your fix of the magic pills, try communicating with her first. You may find that you don't need the pills.

Two other things that relate to impotence or the loss of power are diet and physical activity. During our "Men Only" talk sessions, as we were discussing impotence, I have a friend who is a medical doctor, and he has shared a lot of insight on how what we put in our body affects our ability to perform. Also, regular exercise helps increase the blood flow, and with a good amount of blood flow in the right area, you become as potent as you were when you were eighteen.

Men vs. Abuse

Now for the really hard things that we as men, for whatever reasons, have evaded. Reports indicate that rape and sexual abuse are more frequent and common than we as men want to imagine. I think it is important that we as men take a more active role on denouncing this abusive behavior. Since rarely are the assailants of women other women or the attackers of girls other girls, we must face the fact that "men" are perpetrating these acts of evil. Not only are men predators of women, but also predators of boys, and sometimes even other men.

While we may want to believe that only certain types of men are acting out these vile behaviors, it is not so. Reports indicate that men of every socio-economic level have been found to be sex predators on females and males from infants to senior citizens. Let's address our hard issues as men and stop covering for those who give us a bad name.

I am not advising that we take our baseball bats to the streets and start beating those guys who have been accused of abusing a woman or a child. But we can combat these violent acts by becoming more aware of the facts and effects of domestic violence and abuse in our communities. We can take a

> We can take a more active role in educating our young men about respecting our women and young girls.

more active role in educating our young men about respecting our women and young girls.

If you are a perpetrator of the abuse, you should seek help immediately. Do not become a victim yourself to the cliche that you have an anger management problem. If that was really the case, you would go upside your boss's head every time he upset you, or the cop who issued you the $250 speeding ticket that made you so upset. In each case, you were upset but did not strike them with your fist because you considered the consequences. That dispels the myth that you have an anger management problem.

I acknowledge that I do not know all the facts of your particular situation, so I may sound as if I am being judgmental or self-righteous. However, that is not the case because we all have our issues. It is just that I am tired of turning on the news or picking up a newspaper and seeing where another man has victimized a woman or a girl. Not only are the victims' lives devastated, but now we have lost another man while we are trying to help save a dying generation of young men.

So, my brother, it is my hope that if you are a perpetrator you will find guidance in the following scriptures and seek the professional counseling that I mentioned earlier.

> **Be not hasty in thy spirit to be angry: for anger resteth in the bosom of fools.**
>
> **Ecclesiastes 7:9**

> **But now ye also put off all these; anger, wrath, malice, blasphemy, filthy communication out of your mouth.**
>
> **Colossians 3:8**

We acknowledge that we are naturally highly sexual creatures, stimulated by sight and even fantasies – pictures and movies that we create in our minds. We are very similar biologically, but we are very different physiologically. There is little difference in the shape of the letter X and the letter Y, but that minor difference makes all the difference in the world between the nature of a man and a woman when it comes to the shape of a chromosome. At conception we start out looking the same, but soon we take on real differences, which I've noticed only increase as life goes on.

The male hormone, testosterone, produces many different thoughts and actions in men than in women. With the exception of a small percentage of women, men are most often less emotional and expressive, but are more aggressive, physical, and sexual than women.

Men commit more violent crimes than women, and more men are in jail or prison than women. However, it is said that the fastest growing prison population in our country right now is women. A lot of this can be attributed to the fact that most women in prison are there because of crimes they committed with men or against men.

Most females addicted to drugs and alcohol were first introduced to it and supplied with it by males. Domestic violence is the leading cause of death for women in the United States. One out of three girls is molested or raped by a man, and one of four boys is molested or raped by a man. News reports occasionally indicate that elderly women are even raped in their homes and nursing homes by men.

As a man, again I have to say that it is time for those of us who are not "afflicted" with these behaviors to take a stand against them and put other men on notice before one of our daughters, sons, sisters, mothers, brothers, girlfriends, or wives become a victim.

It has been said, "Silence gives consent." Men in general have been so silent about offenses committed by other men that we have in essence inferred that their crimes against women and children are okay. Were it not for laws against assault and murder, virtually no one would cry "foul."

What We Must Do

The bottom line is that the male sexual nature is nothing to be ashamed of in its proper context. Men always have and always will desire sex more than the average woman. As women come to understand that and we men come to accept it unapologetically, then sex becomes less dirty and less perverted.

However, we as men must take the lead in an effort to clean up our own behavior and image. We must take a pronounced stand against abuse and perversion. We must take the responsibility to resist the temptations to think with the wrong "head" as the quote opening this chapter alluded to. It is our personal responsibility to contain ourselves and not harm or offend anyone else.

Men, we need to take the responsibility to teach our children what appropriate and inappropriate touching is. We need to be the ones to teach our children that there are bad people in the world, and some of them are bad men. We need to be the ones to teach our daughters and our sons that sometimes adults will lie to them in order to take advantage of them. Men need to tell their daughters that boys and men will tell them how pretty they are and how much they love them only to rape and molest them for their own perverse desires.

Men, we need to alert our sons that it is not okay for a man to shower with them, sleep with them, or touch them inappropriately. Simply teach our children and every child we have frequent contact with that anything anyone does to them or tells them and they say it is "a secret," or threaten to harm them or someone they love if they tell, that's the very thing they need to tell *immediately*. They need to tell more than one adult, because unfortunately, not every adult will help them.

We need to stop being so ashamed about the nature of sex that we leave our families vulnerable to sexual predators and abusers. We teach our children more of what to do in case of a fire when the likelihood that they will be sexually accosted before they are eighteen is far more likely.

Nature and time send us cues on when a child should no longer need help dressing, bathing, or sitting on our laps. This is not to say that girls and women who feel comfortable with their fathers who have never been inappropriate with them will not want to sit on dad's lap and give him a hug from time to time. Women like to retain a part of themselves that feels like a little girl, loved and protected by dad. Far too many women do not have safe and loving dads to remember, for they were sexually, physically, and/or emotionally abused by their fathers or men in their lives.

Men, I am telling you, we can be and should be the ones to stop sexual, physical, and emotional abuse of women and children. We start by "checking" each other in our conversations. We need to address things that sound wrong when we hear them and not "silently consent."

We must begin to let other men know that wrong is wrong. Notice how we get to talking about life, work, and family. When a man indicates that he is cheating on his wife, we never discourage him and too often we encourage men as if "that's just what men do" as women and men have said for centuries. Of course, not too often will a man just come out and say, "I am cheating on my wife." Whenever a man does admit that to anyone in those terms, a psychologist would say that he is really asking for help.

I realize that it can be quite difficult at times to confront another man about his issues when you are confronting your own, and I definitely don't want to come across as THE MORAL VOICE FOR MEN, as we all have some secret issues in our lives that we are facing, have faced, or will be facing. But we have to be our brother's keeper and save our generation of dying marriages, families, and MEN.

➤ "We don't really go that far into other people, even when we think we do. We hardly ever go in and bring them out. We just stand at the jaws of the cave and strike a match, and ask quickly if anybody is there."

Martin Amis

Chapter Three

Men and Relationships

As men, there are many different relationships we engage in: parents, siblings, male and female friendships, co-workers, girlfriends, wives, and children. Although relationships are as old as Adam and Eve, we all still have difficulty with them.

I want to address the toughest one first – women. If you are like most of us, you have heard a lot of information about women – their likes, their dislikes, how to get a woman, how to please a woman, how to please a woman in bed, how to get a woman to please you in bed, and on and on. You have probably even read several articles about how to deal with women.

If you are having significant and consistent problems dealing with women and you have not read a good article about women – I mean an article in a magazine that did not come in a paper wrapper with a viewing warning on the label – then let this be the start of your new education about women.

Rules May Not Apply

First, you need to know that most of the information you may have read about how sensitive and emotionally different women are than men, is true. Most of the information you have heard about how women enjoy talking and shopping is true. The tension, moodiness, and sensitivity women often experience during their menstrual cycles are natural and temporary. Even the dreaded menopause of middle-aged women with hot flashes and edginess is often true.

However, gentlemen, I promised the women I know that I would tell you to remember that while there are some basic rules and similarities, all women are not the same.

Just think of the variances in the women you have known. Some liked sports, some did not. Some were great cooks, others couldn't boil water. Some liked the outdoors, others hated it. Some were super neat while others could care less. Some cost you a lot of money, others were cheap dates.

Some men get frustrated easily because everything they thought they learned from their previous girlfriends sometimes does not work with their new girlfriend. That is really kind of silly when you think about it, because if you wished that the new girlfriend was like the last one, or even the first girlfriend, then why did you break it off with either of them and all of those in between?

Having said that, the most common problem in male-female relationships is that they often expect one to think like the other. That may sound great at first, but think it through and see how weird that would be. Imagine someone just like you – with breasts and a menstrual cycle. Even people who enjoy being by themselves want someone different to talk to sometimes.

I know I can really appreciate the differences between me and my wife. I have always had the tendency to be the kind of guy who is in a hurry to get things done – so much so that I was never a great planner. I felt that planning slowed me down.

On the other hand, my wife carefully plans out everything before making a move. After watching her do this effectively for sixteen years, I thought I'd try it. Guess what? It works! Did you really think I would write a book and not find a place to compliment my wife? Are you crazy?!

Now, back to the point that as much as you love hanging out with your best buddy – fishing, watching the games, playing basketball or a round of golf – you get tired of being with another fellow like yourself. If you don't, then you may fall into another category of men I talked about in chapter 2 on "Men and Sex."

If you are a regular heterosexual guy, soon you will want a little "female company." Not just sex – that too – but we just simply enjoy looking at "beautiful" women, chatting with them, smelling their perfume, and watching them walk that certain way that women do. We especially love their attention and affection when we finally win one of our own.

So the next time you are about to gripe that she does not appreciate the big game like you do or that she doesn't know the difference between an inning, a quarter, or a half, remember the alternative is to be without her – all of her. A great quote someone shared says, "If we are both the same, then one of us is unnecessary."

One thing that will make us more successful in our relationships, since we cannot actually think like women, is to try to listen and understand them more. If you have ever tried to communicate with someone who does not speak English, and you thought that if you were able to get them to speak a little more slowly, then perhaps you could read their lips, only to realize how silly that was. Then you have the beginning of improving the communication in your relationship.

I am sure you found out what worked best in that situation was to watch the other person's gestures and facial expressions more than anything they tried to tell you. By watching their movements, we were able to perceive much more than we had time to consult our book of translations to find the words individually.

The next basic tool in improving our relationships is to try to wear the other person's shoes. Not just women. I say this more generally because as men, we can be very cavalier about how we treat others when we are tired, rushed, or upset. This may sound rather simple or soft, but many men realize after the tenth failed relationship that they are not doing something well.

One other seemingly simple mistake we often make is to "get in a hurry." When I get a chance to talk to single men, in particular, I have noticed that often their common "lapse in judgment" is that they get in a hurry in a new relationship. If a woman does not produce the specific things they want in a woman right away, then they tend to quickly move on to the next.

> Men, do not forget that a woman is like a car in winter. If you want her to drive well, you need to give her a little time to warm up properly.

Men, do not forget that a woman is like a car in winter. If you want her to drive well, you need to give her a little time to warm up properly. If you rush in and think that she is going to do and be all that she really is in the first week or so, you may miss out on the woman of your dreams.

◆ "THE YOUNG MAN WHO HAS NOT WEPT IS A SAVAGE, AND THE OLD MAN WHO WILL NOT LAUGH IS A FOOL."

GEORGE SANTAYANA

Chapter Four

Men and Emotions

While women have a full array of emotions and they use them all, men have a full array of emotions also. Women just seem to have at least four times more than men. However, as men, we tend to limit ourselves to happy, sad, angry, glad, and frustrated. Regardless of the extremity of the emotion, we modestly relegate it to one of these categories and indicate the degree of intensity by preceding the emotion with, "I am very," or "I am not." This makes expression very easy and concise for us.

Anger, the Default Emotion

"Anger makes dull men witty, but it keeps them poor."

Francis Bacon

Since we are addressing "the hard things that men never talk about," I'll cut straight to the chase and talk about our most problematic emotion – anger. Each time we hold "Men Only" sessions, someone asks how to manage or stop his anger. This very strongly suggests to me that men sometimes know when they have an anger problem and they want to be free of it.

After consulting analysts and professionals in the field of human behavior, they all point to two most common root causes of anger. It almost sounds too simple, but at the source of all anger is actually hurt. Psychoanalysts rely on information from a person's history to diagnose and treat current behavior.

Studies from some of the most violent criminals in the penal system indicate that most of them suffered some form of severe abuse or neglect they can recall from as young as ages three and four years old to their teen years. The hurt and pain from the abuse and neglect they experienced in their young lives have spilled over in the form of crime, violence, and perversion. They have learned and/or developed a lack of respect for life and others. Many of them have actually mimicked the same offenses perpetrated on them, or repeated what they grew up watching at home and in their neighborhoods.

Criminal and violent behavior to the point of incarceration is the extreme. However, there are many more angry men living among us in society than are in jails and prisons.

Hidden Frustration

The second primary cause of anger is "frustration." A good friend of mine says that in her studies, she has found that men and women who have difficulty expressing themselves, or who suppress frustration and have compiled disappointment, often act out in a continuous stream of anger or sudden outbursts. Their "daily anger" or their continuous stream of anger, seems inexplicable to those who live and work with them.

Sudden angry outbursts may even seem unprovoked and unrelated to current events. This is called "displaced anger," and it manifests itself in various forms. Since most of us are not psychiatrists or psychologists, we do not make such assessments or make the connections as readily. So typically those around an angry person simply react or suffer through it as it comes.

Ending Anger

The first step to dealing with anger from frustration is to sit down and figure out "what is really bugging you." Men who tend to downplay and ignore their emotions, typically need help from some concerned, safe person who will help them "talk" and dig within themselves for deep introspection until they find their root irritant.

Once again, the importance of being able to communicate, verbalize, and articulate what you are going through is vital. We need to have enough words in our vocabulary to be able to communicate our wants and needs, and to say what hurts us and where it hurts so we can end the pain and get wants and needs met.

In chapter 1, I addressed "communication" specifically. You may want to review that chapter again if you have an anger problem as a start to ending your anger. You may want to consult your pastor if he is a trained or experienced counselor or a trained professional counselor to get further help.

Imagine that you have your hand tightly over the water faucet, then you turn the water on just a little. Soon the water will seep through your fingers because of the cracks in your hand, and because the water is on, it is coming out and can't go back.

Now, imagine that you have the water on at full pressure. Not only does it come through your hand, it sprays everywhere and makes a huge mess. Also, the force is so great that you cannot keep a grip on it.

The pressure of anger has the same effect. It can only be contained briefly, and then it seeps through, or bursts through. The pressure of frustration comes on more like a silent drip that you don't hear until a lot of water (frustration) has accumulated. Then, that slow drip goes on for a while until it floods the whole bathroom and seeps through walls, doors, and the floor below, if possible.

Fulfillment

Fulfillment is the sense of gratification you get from the things you do that make you feel good about having accomplished it, or gives you pleasure from having produced it. Your source of fulfillment may have no relevance or any real meaning to anyone else.

For example, building a ship in a bottle may give you a real sense of fulfillment, but it is of little value to anyone else. However, each time you see it mounted and completed, you get a sense of accomplishment from it. You feel somewhat immortalized and spoken for. No one appreciates your ship in the bottle as much as you do.

But if they took time to realize what really went into it and the time you spent on it, perhaps they would see the value in it. They just see a ship in a bottle. They may appreciate how well it is constructed, but they don't see the peace and solitude you needed and found in building it. It became your retreat, your getaway from stress and strain. Often while building it, you were able to make major decisions for your life and family while enjoying the peace and solitude.

> Building a ship in a bottle is rather indicative of life. You do not supply the pieces, but you do have to put them together.

A Ship in a Bottle

Building a ship in a bottle is rather indicative of life. You do not supply the pieces, but you do have to put them together. There are instructions, but you do not have to follow them. You can just look at the picture and think that you can figure it out on your own, but you will probably end up with a mess. If you make a few mistakes early, you may be able to start over. But if you make too many mistakes later, you are probably stuck with them. The opening is very narrow. Only one hand can operate and build there at a time. Regardless of what you build in the bottle, others can see it clearly when you are done.

Picasso painted for the sake of fulfillment and peace, not for money. Painting soothed the passion of his raging soul. As a child he was told that he had no talent. It was not until he fulfilled his need to paint that he realized that others valued his fulfillment. While he was alive, he was paid well for his paintings. After his death, his work became priceless because there would not be another Picasso – and there will never be another you!

Passion

"Death is the only pure, beautiful conclusion of a great passion."

D. H. Lawrence

Passion is the insatiable desire you have for something or someone. Passion is often incomprehensible to everyone else "not of like passion." Bishop Jakes once described passion as "the thing you would do for free." This is true. Once you have discovered what your passion is, you get so much fulfillment and satisfaction from doing it that you are not as concerned with the compensation that comes from doing it. At least in the beginning.

However, there are two major concerns I have about our passion as men. First, the ability to find our passion. This really is not a problem isolated to just men. Women have some difficulty too. I think we have difficulty finding our passion because most of us find things to do that we must do and not things to do that we enjoy doing.

Many of us were asked as children, "What do you want to do when you grow up?" Most of us did not know. The unfortunate thing is, too many of us grow up and never really know or try to find it until much later in life. I know older men who still reminisce about what they wish they could have done. So I encourage you to consider finding and pursuing your passion. Search within yourself for that thing that comes naturally to you but seems to really be a challenge for everyone else.

Some would say that what I have just described is a gift and that is true, but it is your passion for it that allows you to do it for hours and not even notice the time go by. You go to bed thinking of it and it's your first thought upon waking up in the morning.

Now, I hope you realize that I am not talking about sex. That may be one of your passions, but that is not what I am speaking of right now. Seriously, let's really consider this because far too many of us have played around and tried to sex and game our way through the questions:

- **What was I placed here to do?**
- **What void will I fill in the earth?**

We seem to only reflect on these questions in the winter of our lives when we no longer have the energy, zeal, resources, and/or a strong desire to bring the answer to these questions into existence. So, my brother, start today asking and finding the answers to these questions, for then you will experience your greatest joy.

Second, I am concerned with our ability to control our passion. I discussed much about controlling rage and sexual desire in previous chapters. So I will only mention that we must become more mindful of control. Not control in a negative sense of manipulation, but in the sense of managing ourselves better.

I am concerned that for the vast majority of us, even we have found the answers to the questions posed above, we give up on ourselves too easily.

"Anything worth having is worth working for."

Most of us have heard the old adage, "Anything worth having is worth working for." We readily do this when it comes to working for someone else, but rarely are we willing to commit time to study and prepare to develop our talents and gifts.

Once you have discovered your passion, there will be a degree of preparation needed to ultimately propel to what it is you were created to do. I dare not claim to know anyone's passion other than my own, my wife's, and currently, I am helping my three children find theirs. But I do know whatever you are to do, it will require some level of preparation and dedication. Part of the preparation is reading material on what it is you feel you were placed here to do, getting to know people in that arena and study them, and last but certainly not least, taking care of your health. You don't want to be prepared mentally and have your health fail you.

➤ "A father is a gift from God from which we learn to be patient, strong, and loving, filled with integrity."
　　　　　Byron P. Tousingant

➤ "There is no more vital calling or vocation for men than fathering."
　　　　　John R. Throop
　　　　　Parents and Children

➤ "Nothing I've ever done has given me more joys and rewards than being a father to my five."
　　　　　Bill Cosby
　　　　　Fatherhood

➤ "The words a father speaks to his children in the privacy of the home are not overheard at the time, but as in whispering galleries, they will be heard at the end by posterity."
　　　　　Jean Paul Richter

Chapter Five

Men – As Fathers

To be a father is one of the greatest joys a man can have in his life. There is something beyond what words can explain about seeing your child, your own flesh and blood, for the first time. A flood of thoughts and emotions goes through your mind. You are proud and scared, excited and nervous, at the same time. Within minutes the weight and responsibility of it all seem to tap you on the shoulder. You inhale as if to say, "I'm a dad now. I can handle this."

Regardless of how rich or not so rich you are, the sense of responsibility for a new life overshadows you at that moment. However, the awesomeness of what has just taken place overshadows your practical thoughts or anxiety about affording and raising a child or another child.

> There is something about having a child that seems to add quality and value to your life.

There is something about having a child that seems to add quality and value to your life. You now have a new and rejuvenated reason to live and succeed. There is a sense of pride about having part of yourself replicated in the earth that is different from what even mothers experience. Before you can walk out of the hospital, you seem to walk taller and your chest swells with pride and joy.

Whatever man you were before the delivery of your first child, you became someone else in addition to who you were. I want to acknowledge that as wonderful as this is, it is not true for all men, and I will address "reluctant fathers" later in this chapter.

The Joy of Responsibility

Most often we focus on the responsibility of being a father. We all know that being a father has its responsibility. But typically when we talk about the "R" word, it is in the negative sense. I want to flip the coin and look at "the joy of responsibility."

You can ask any viable business owner about the difficulty of being in business, and he will tell you, "Yes, it is really hard to have your own business and there is a lot of responsibility, but it is so rewarding."

That's what I think being a father is like. There is a lot of stress and strain sometimes. You will lose some sleep when they cry at night and it's your turn to heat the bottle. You will be amazed at the cost of their little diapers, formula, and the clothes they outgrow every month, but you cannot replace the joy they bring. It is a package deal – joy and responsibility – but so is everything in life that is worth having.

As I pay attention to what is important to men, nine out of ten times the first that is mentioned on their list is their kids, if they have children. You may not have as much time with your children as their mother has in the first years of their lives, but you will want to capture and cherish every moment that you can get because you will never have that moment again. Some of the funniest things you will never forget will be something your kids did. You will do some of the silliest things you ever dreamed of just for fun with your kids.

You have never known pure, unadulterated, unconditional love until your little child wraps those little arms around your legs, clinging on for dear life just because he or she is glad to see you come home from work. There is nothing like the smile and pleadings of a child that will make you drag your exhausted bag of bones, after working extra hours, out of your favorite chair just to toss a ball around the yard, or teach him or her to ride a bike without training wheels. Some of the most exhausting and most gratifying days I have had were spent with my children.

Fathers of older and grown children often say there were some trying times in raising their children, but they tend to emphasize the joy and pride they have in their children over any challenges they had to face.

"My father was not a failure. After all, he was the father of a President of the United States."

Harry S. Truman

The Road to Destiny

Fathers are like maps. They tell you where you are, where you came from, and where you can go if you get good directions. Someone once said, "Without knowing one's point of origin, how can one know where he is going or when he has arrived?"

While fathers have not always gotten the recognition for the imperative role they play in the lives of their children, the "fallout" from single-parent homes with mothers only has turned national and international interest on fathers. Studies prove all sorts of dysfunctions in society point back to unstable and fatherless homes.

Actually, you do not need studies to see the decay of individuals and homes. You need only visit your nearest public school, urban area, jail, or drug treatment center to draw your own conclusions. The effects of fatherless homes are not only apparent in urban or inner-city areas. Wealthy children of single-parent homes headed by women have very similar dysfunctions. They are simply better financed.

Historically, a child was presented as a gift from a wife to a husband, especially if the child was a son. In previous centuries, fathers also most often named their children. Not only did they give them the all-important family name, they also frequently chose their first names as well. Shakespeare said, "What is in a name?" The answer is, "A lot"! Just ask anyone who got a bad one; i.e., Jabez (KJV).

While few namesakes appreciate being a "Jr." or if you prefer, a "II" or a "III," unless they are the heir to a throne, there is a sense of pride and belonging to be named after your father. One of the most significant spaces on birth certificates is "father's name." When most anyone sees their birth certificate for the first time, after they check the spelling of their name, they check the name in that little box which says who their father is.

It can be rather disheartening to find "unknown" in that box, when quite obviously no one has been produced without a "father" – no one on earth or in heaven. So we know that for every birth certificate, there is a father somewhere.

Some fathers are not as active or visible in their children's lives as other fathers are. Whether fathers actively guide or passively lead, they become a form of compass for their children's lives.

One of my friends likes to say, "Sometimes the best thing anyone can teach you is what *not* to do." So whether you have a great father or an absent or distant father, you learned something from him. Most of us decided what type of parent we wanted to be when we grew up based upon the type of parent(s) we had. Few of us meet that goal, but it makes for a good conscious effort.

The ability to produce a child is not enough to call yourself a "father." You must provide for the physical, emotional, and spiritual needs of your children to fill the shoes of fatherhood. Fathers nurture their children differently than mothers, and in a way that is badly needed. It is the difference between "real fathers" and "biological fathers." I know we have heard this for a couple of decades now, but apparently we have not heard it enough yet.

Many people grow up without ever meeting their biological fathers. They may even have really good stepfathers, grandfathers, or surrogate fathers, but they always have a large or small void in their lives from not knowing who their own father is.

"What is a father? To his child, he is strength, security, example, and number one friend. It's a great calling, so celebrate the gift of your fatherhood!"

Reluctant Fathers

Many of us entered into fatherhood unplanned and before we were "ready." Many times we were just trying to have "a little fun" and ended up fathers. Of course, not all men were ready to become fathers and not all fathers were ready to become men. In far too many instances, males become "biological fathers" and virtual "sperm donors" instead of fathers.

Whether you chose to become a father or you just happened upon it, it is a defining moment in your life. From the moment a woman tells you that she is pregnant with your child, your response defines what you are made of. If you immediately become skeptical about the paternity of the child, it speaks of the kind of woman you have chosen to risk your life and future with. If you immediately become concerned about how having a baby will negatively affect your life over everyone and everything else involved, that says you thought too late and you are likely to be too self-absorbed to parent properly. If you become paralyzed with shock or fear, that says you probably should not have sex again until you better understand the correlation between sex and conception.

If you have shock and joy at the news, you are likely to make a good father. From the time you get the news, over the next eight to nine months, you have time to prepare and define or redefine yourself. It becomes a time of quick and deep reflection about where you are and where you want to go.

"As soon as you become a father, your job is cut out for you. It is probably the most eternally significant job you will ever have."

Paul Heidebrecht
Parents and Children

Play Time Is Over

Whether you were age fifteen or thirty when you got the news that you had a baby on the way, you knew that "play time was over." I don't mean that you expected to never have fun again. Perhaps some of you did, but whatever you were wasting time doing while not taking life very seriously, suddenly changed. Suddenly manhood came crashing down on you, whether you accepted it or not. If you ever spent much time wondering if you wanted to have children or ever would have children, your question is over. While fatherhood is not the end of fun in your life, it definitely does change when, where, and how you have that fun.

If you have been "living on the fly," just any-'ol-kind-of-way, you now must decide to find stability, decide the role you will play in your child's life, decide whether marriage is an option, or decide to opt out of your child's life.

You may need to think about getting a job if you do not have one, getting a better job, finding a new place to live, and perhaps even trading your motorcycle or two-seater for something you can put a car seat in. If you have a busy lifestyle, or your job involves a lot of travel, you then have to plan to adapt your schedule, not to mention adjusting your expenses to meet new financial needs. That's just a given.

If you are a father, recognize that you are your children's point of reference and starting line. Whatever you say or do will inevitably affect your children for the rest of their lives to a greater or lesser degree. What you say to your children is one of the most defining life-giving or life-destroying roles you will ever play in their lives, second only to any form of neglect or abuse.

◆ "Money doesn't talk, it swears."
  Bob Dylan

◆ "Nothing links man to man like the frequent passage from hand to hand of cash."
  Walter Sickert

◆ "Money can't buy you friends, but you can get a better class of enemies."
  Spike Milligan

Chapter Six

Men and Money

Just saying "men and money" conjures up so many thoughts in your mind and is such a powerful subject that of course we are going to talk about it. Some seem to think that men have an unusual affinity for money. I agree that our view of money is sometimes different from that of women. Perhaps it is because we have traditionally been the primary "providers" for our families since the beginning of life as we know it.

We can admit that there are and have been many instances where men have allowed greed to cause them to cross lines and cause harm to many. Some men use money as a base to build their self-esteem. Some not only build a base for it, but the pedestals too for lifting themselves up above the crowd. However, for most men, the pursuit of money is not just a challenge or an ego trip, it is a simple necessity. I want to talk about our attitudes and efforts towards money and using money.

First Money

"So you think money is the root of all evil. Have you ever asked what is the root of money?"

Ayn Rand

Money is so imperative to the quality of everyone's life that it is really unfortunate that most people do not have enough of it and others have more than they can spend. The first thing I want to do is to encourage you to "get more of it." With more you can certainly do more. Financial stability gives you the option to right some of the wrongs in our society and certainly provides a better future for your family. So it's a given that we must work hard and smart to acquire more of it.

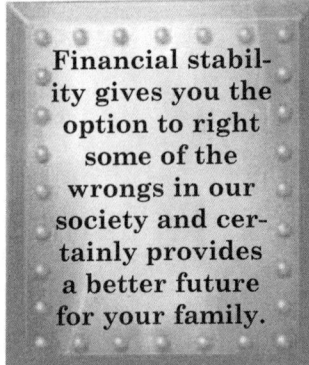

However, one of the mistakes we seem to make today as parents, and especially fathers, is that we are not teaching our children, especially our sons, how to "work hard" anymore. Obviously, this 21st century is a technological age, and many jobs do not require as much physical labor as in previous generations.

So in saying "work hard," I don't mean just physical labor. I mean that we need to be sure that we teach our children the importance of working "for" something and not just having everything handed to them.

Most parents enjoy giving their children things that their parents could not afford to give them as children and we should do that. But, while we are "blessing" our children on the one hand, we are crippling them on the other. We must learn to love them without spoiling them and "ruining" them by not teaching them now to be goal oriented and tenacious. It is important that every child learns this because most of them are not born into wealth, and some of those who are will not be able to keep it. So we need to prepare our children to know how to survive in case life gets hard, as it is prone to do. When our children learn to work for money, we do not have to worry so much about their future as adults.

Someone coined the phrase, "Work smart, not hard." It was an effort towards encouraging people to use their minds more than their muscles, but I prefer to think that "hard work" can be just as smart as "soft work" for anyone who chooses it. There is nothing wrong with physical labor if that's what you like, or have to do to earn a living.

There is nothing like a little "sweat equity" to make us appreciate what we have. It is an experience I believe every capable young man, and even some young women, should have in order to appreciate "soft work" because money really does not grow on trees and there are no genies in a bottle! Most of us still have to work for money. The sooner we begin to teach our children about money, the more successful they will be at getting it and keeping it.

Does Money Make the Man?

Does money really make the man? Some people seem to think so. Because life is so limited without money, some men virtually live to make money. There are so many options to life when money is not a problem. You can choose to live virtually anyplace, you can drive what you want, and buy what you want. You can travel and see the country, see the world, and have many, many more options.

Money does not make the man, but money certainly makes life easier and causes you to see your life differently. While money is a necessity, I think that it is important that we differentiate ourselves, our personhood, from money so as not to become confused about who we are based upon our bank accounts.

Obviously, there are fewer men in America who are actually "wealthy." Most of us are just comfortable or barely breaking even. There are few differences between men who have money, who have a lot of money, and who have less money than they would like, but those differences are huge. Men with less money tend to have a different perspective of themselves. They may have strength and confidence, but it is often more physical and aggressive, brute strength and a cocky attitude that give them that strength and confidence when money is scarce or absent.

The ego of a man is vital. The ego is our struggle for and perception of ourselves. So often, when we cannot feed our ego one way, we find another way to stand out, even in an audience of one. Often, I try to find the differences that make one man drink and yell on an open street corner, who is poorly dressed and dirty; and another man, well-groomed, who quietly goes along his way.

One of the differences is where they get their esteem and ego fed. For the man yelling on the street corner, all he has at the moment to get attention and feed his ego is to make a spectacle of himself, as if to say, "Look at me." For the other man, it is his job, home, and being able to provide for himself and/or his family, among other things no doubt, that build his self-esteem. One is no more or less a man, but the differences are huge.

Of course, the thousands of differences in where they grew up, who their parents were, where they went to school, how much education they received, who their friends were, all of their experiences and on and on, caused the sum total of the person they became.

Men with fewer opportunities and finances often have equal ego needs. So, in order to achieve the esteem their ego needs, some men may do things that other men would never do, and those choices are often financially based.

Men with Money

"Money is a singular thing. It ranks with love as man's greatest source of joy and with death as man's greatest source of anxiety. Money differs from an automobile, a mistress, or cancer in being equally important to those who have it and those who do not."

J. K. Galbraith

Men with money identify themselves differently than men without money. Men with money seem to have a strength that tends to be more psychological and assertive. Their boldness tends to be more from confidence, or even arrogance, than a man without very much money. Men with money can do more, buy more, and go more places. Men with money rule the world, but that's about the extent of it. Once again, there are only a few differences, but those differences are huge.

However, I focus on our common issues as men. We all worry about our manhood at some point in our lives. We all give some thought to or panic about thinning or disappearing hair. Also, we are all concerned about dying and whether or not we leave any markers or monuments to signify that we lived.

When you are at the bottom looking up, it is easier to see the advantages that others who "have" get to enjoy. Often, the people with less can appreciate what the wealthy have more than those who have it. It is more difficult for the "haves" on the top to see commonalities with those on the bottom. There is an unfortunate side effect to wealth for many people, especially if they started out poor and ended rich. Too often they lose the ability to relate to the common man. We all deny it, but check our benevolence.

In America no one has to be homeless or hungry. No one. We still will not help our friends not to mention our neighbors. Yes, the poor will be with us always. We have good authority on that, but does it have to be such a large percentage?

Men, Money, and Women

A female colleague of mine says, "Men too often think that all women want from them is their money." She said she has turned down several offers to date or to be "kept" by men with substantial money in hopes of finding love and companionship with a man who is at least comfortable and self-sufficient.

Most interesting and appealing women today can support themselves without the help of a man, which leaves some men in a quandary about what to use as bait to lure them. Since we do not really know what about us will attract certain women, men have a great deal more confidence with women when we have money.

First of all, men have to be able to afford to take women out. Then, we have to be able to outdo the next man in impressing a woman. We rely on the fact that if our looks or charm does not work, then money and a nice car will. Even before the advent of money, men were able to acquire women if they had enough property and cattle to afford the dowry.

Interestingly enough, women judge and choose men by so many different variables until we are often mistaken or confused by what they want from us. Some women only cater to men with six figure incomes. Other women place little emphasis on a man's financial status. What is really confusing is that there are some women who seem not to care if a man has a penny to his name and are even willing to finance the "bum," just as long as they have a man.

And certainly when I speak of this, I am not speaking of the brother who has just lost his job or is simply in a temporary state of non-income producing time. The "bum" is the guy who has been in a non-income state for years.

Conclusion

Gentlemen, we have indeed discussed some hard things in this book, and it is my hope that you have been touched and your life changed by what you have read.

Because *Man Talk* is not just about discussing the issues in a man's world but to discuss them in a way that offers solutions and healing, I would be doing an injustice if I didn't talk about one of the things that helps us as we continue on this journey of becoming the man we have been called to be.

You see, one of the few things we talk about as men is *worship,* and frankly, whether we talk about it publicly or not is not as important as making sure that we practice it privately. Worship has to become a vital part of our *DAILY ROUTINE.*

When I speak of worship, I am not speaking of some of the things such as money, sex, pride, and image that we allow to come into our world and set up shop in our lives as gods. I mean communing and having a personal relationship with the only One who can do anything about everything that we have discussed in this book and will ever discuss in the future.

We opened the book with a chapter on communication and the importance of it with women. We even talked about our relationships and how it is important for us to seek ways to improve our relationships with our wives and children. As important as this is, the single most important relationship you will ever have is your relationship with your Creator.

Ultimately, to get the answers to all of the questions that life will ever ask us, men, we have to go back to the One who started it all and that is our Lord and Savior, Jesus the Christ. It is through spending time in His Word, praying, speaking with Him and allowing Him to speak to us through the Holy Spirit, and the godly men and women He has placed in our lives, that we will receive the answers we need.

Sometimes this can be challenging because we equate time to money. It's something we feel we simply don't have enough of so we say we don't have enough time in the day to spend laying before Him and seeking His face. I have found on the days that I don't take time to do this, those seem to be the longest days and the least productive days.

The second thing that stops some of us from doing this is we feel that we have messed up so much that God is not interested in hearing from us. But on the contrary, God wants us to run to Him. First John 1:9 states, **"If we confess our sins, he is faithful and just to forgive us our sins, and to cleanse us from all unrighteousness."** This is not a license to sin, but God in His sovereign grace and infinite wisdom has given us yet another escape from the clutches of the enemy. So don't let anything stop you from seeking that deeper relationship with God and taking time to worship Him.

Prayer of Salvation

Perhaps as you have read this book, you say, "That sounds wonderful, but I don't have a relationship with God nor have I ever had a relationship with Him." Well, my brother, this can be the first day of the rest of your life, for your past mistakes do not dictate future failure.

Please pray the following prayer, and seek out a good Bible-believing and preaching church.

Lord, I confess that I am a sinner. I ask You, Lord, to forgive me of all my sins and wash me with the blood of Jesus Christ. I ask You, Lord, to come into my heart and my life and be my personal Lord and Savior.

Fill me with the Holy Spirit and write my name in the Book of Life. Your Word says that if I confess with my mouth the Lord Jesus and believe in my heart that God has raised Him from the dead, I will be saved. Lord, that is my belief and my confession, so I seal this prayer in faith believing that I am now saved, in Jesus' name. Amen. It is so.

My brothers, this concludes this Man Talk session, but it does not end our conversation about men and the issues in our world. I look forward to seeing you at one of our future Man Talk sessions. Until then, take care of yourself and each other!

For information about Man Talk sessions or to
correspond directly with Chris Howell,
you may contact us:

Online at:
www.mantalkonline.com
www.chrishowellonline.com

Via-Mail:
Chris Howell
P. O. Box 300284
Arlington, TX 76007

The following pages have been intentionally left blank to allow you the opportunity to make notes of the things in this book that you feel will help you become the man you were created to be.

NOTES

NOTES

NOTES